DEDICATION

dedicated to the people who make life worth writing about.

willow

she sways like a willow
who's been ready to fall
and she drinks
like she hopes
it's the cure

she plays my song
but she's too drunk
to sing along
from the doorframe i mouth the words
for her instead

something in the kick drum of
her handpicked melody
reminds me
of the kids we used to be

before medicine became whatever drink
she's sipping now
i'd heal her in a moment
if she'd only show me
how

and when she falls in front of me
i'll catch her in my arm

she's a mess but still an angel in
her purple petal dress

she can't hide the tears that start
to spill
but she tries to play along
so i hold her while she's hurting
and i'll keep her
till it's gone

sarah bork, tim roth 1991

two faces
suspended in grain
a photograph hung
on the wall

he wears a smirk
and a denim shirt
and she laughs at
the words on his tongue

she covers her eyes
and squeezes them shut
and her dimples imply
the sound

i can hear it from here
and it echoes the hall
as i stare at the frame
on the wall

thank god for sandria
seeing those two
the same way that i
see them now

and god bless the camera
the utmost companion
for turning two humans
to art

tinkerbell

for the girl at the party
with the blonde hair
black hoodie
and the half full plastic cup

i hope you'll remember my name
and the conversation
we engaged in
standing on the stairs

at every party i'll be looking
for a chance to finish
telling you
i wish i knew the truth

to every implication
that i made
about
your heart

white space

it starts with a line
a passable art
an itch from the muse
that infects every wall inside
my brain

i try to please
the diety
i touch the pen but i
can never get
much farther

than a scribble in ink
a strikethrough the heart
and a page full
of red lines
and white spaces between

sleeping arrangements

i used to think one day
we'd both grow up and fall back in
to the impressions that we left
on my couch

but the cushions couldn't hold our shape
and i know we'll never have
the love
i tried
but couldn't make

i'll leave your voice inside the message
you left for me
before that
friday night

and your body in my memory
on the bathroom floor
your freckled face
secure between my
hands

red velvet

i miss the way you laugh
with both your hands
the way
you grab me when you laugh
too hard to stand

it's the width of your lips
when you smile
the little things
the curvature
of both your freckled cheeks

but more than that
i miss when we were friends
and you were still
the girl from down the street

and i don't think i can love you
now
when i'm still in love
with who you used to be

loon song

there's a bird out on the water
somewhere in
the fog
he calls the lake for company
but i've never heard
the sound
i start to wonder why he floats
the ocean
on his own

i mourn the empty place she left
beside me
on the couch we called a bed
but there'd be no grief
if i'd been the one
to pack my heart
and go

either way
i understand
why the loon sings alone
i'm a romantic
but i sleep pretty well
on my own

nobody

the world looks a little smaller
with my head against
her chest

her steady breathing
fills the silence
and the music says
the rest

moonlight filters through the blinds
i see her lovely nose
and perfect lips

and if the world would end tonight
i think i'd be content
if she
were it

yellow headed blackbird

i wonder if the ducks
saw our walk along the shoreline
if the geese could see the way i watched you
throwing rocks across
the water

and the blackbirds perched on reeds that
screamed at
me repeatedly
told me things about you
that we both
already knew

i won't love you
once i leash my heart
from chasing cars
i know
i'll never
catch

spectral

i called her crystal earrings
accents
to the finest piece of art
i'd ever seen
the room was spinning but
her eyes
anchored me down

my toe was bruised from the careless shoes
of the party above
our heads
and when she kissed it she blessed it with
a lovely metaphor
that i could hide in any bathroom
but no matter where
she'd still notice
my pain

she doesn't find me on the floor
anymore
but i still wait for her
to come through
that door
and the last thing i see before
my consciousness

retreats
a pair of crystal earrings
without
their lovely
host

chicago

i gave you my favorite sweatshirt
to keep you warm
against
the last snowstorm
of march

i took you home
you wore it inside
and i
pretended not to notice

just friends don't take each others
clothes
i could've kept it but i
guess that i
forgot

despite the times you taught me otherwise
i still have
a tendency
of giving what i know
i'll never
get

but i like the way you look in my crewneck

and i hope it keeps you
warm
on coldest days
in the summer of
chicago

the empress

16

her hands are cool when she holds mine in them
a foreign temperature
to remind my skin
of the presence of another body
sometimes it scares me
to be reminded what
she's capable of
when i let her touch me

tin man

through the birch trees
i see
the tin man
his axe held high above his head

in agony
the moment before he carries out his swing
stretches on
suspended in a demonstration of his strength

his shoulders
carry the capability
of wielding such a tool
but his body denies him
the chance

to perform
any function that would separate himself
from the lifeless tangled trees
that surround him

i recognize the torment in his eyes
like windows
that regard me
with the same pity

i hold
for him

he's a man
with a mind the body won't obey
and here i stand
his perfect inversion

i try my best
but with every hollow word i write
my muscles seize
and discourage the movements of
my pen

the muse never speaks to me anymore
the axe
never swings
anymore

the gardener

the spade slices through
his skin
and sows seeds of every color
his flesh becomes
the soil

i want to take his pain
away
to dam the river from his eyes
with rocks to stop
the flow
but the seeds need water
to grow

one day he'll see the flowers
that grew from wounds
i wish he never
had to bear
but what a greater tragedy it would be
to deprive the world
of the beauty
that grew
from his pain

hunter

he looks in the mirror
and waits
for his sentence
his eyes are shadowed in blue

the judgment falls
on his shoulders
and the voice of his father
repeats

the words of a man
weigh on the heart
of a boy
with paint on his hands

he looks in the mirror and considers himself
worthy
despite
the eyes
of the judge

quorra

to have been held by someone
as beautiful
as the way it felt to learn to love
again
is a memory i'd
never be
as whole if i forgot

pruning

hate doesn't flow from my fingers
the same way
that love does

it starts in my stomach
and climbs through my veins
and clogs my brain like rotted leaves
caught inside a
rain gutter

i never wrote about what
you did to me
but it doesn't change
the fact

it doesn't heal the severed stems
of saplings
that had barely started
to grow

i still love the ways you proved you could be
beautiful
but that doesn't mean
i'm finished clearing
the stumps you left
behind

lamplight

she's dancing in the lamplight
and i get to witness
from the back row

she's twirling and her tassels are soaring as she
spins
and her smile beams down like the spotlight that
attaches to
her body

but behind that smile
both of us know
that tonight is the last night she'll ever dance on
a stage

i wish all the flowers could fix her
that carnations were
the cure.

she's celebrating her legs before the stitches in
her hips
come undone
and it's breaking my heart to watch

the beauty of the moment before the curtain falls

like a star burns brightest before it goes
dim

she's just a girl who's dancing
before
the beauty
dies

yes i still think about

that yellow thistle flower
that you left on the edge of the hill

but the way you look at him reminds me
how she looked at me before

she pulled my broken heart out
and she left it on the floor

i like you but my neck will break
from one more silver medal

the reception

it's almost been a year since
the wedding
the memory hasn't left my head
you wore a black dress
which seemed to match the tone of the reception
all those people but the drinks were
just for us
i spent my whole life preparing for the day when
i would turn down the offer
but in the end it was a low cut
pursed lips
and pink eyeshadow that broke me
you were the most fun i'd ever had in my life
and when you kissed me and told me you loved
me
i was well aware
of your state of mind when i replied and said
i loved you
too
that night on the typewriter i wrote the best thing
that i'd ever written
and i wrote it for you
jules
and when you said you'd be back
i believed you

i kept that picture of you with a shot in your
hand and your eyelids weighed down
relaxed
on the back of my eyelids for months
it's almost been a year since the wedding
and i still haven't seen
your face
but i want to
so i write like it was yesterday
maybe if i reimagine every shade of your irises
or every grain of your skin
i can build you a body i can
love
it's almost been a year since the wedding
and any sober eyes could see
the fact
you're never coming
back

jules

i love you
even though you were drunk when you said it

you said it
i love you

how many drinks will it take
to tell you i wasn't
drunk when i said
i did too

before i go

Nate Brown

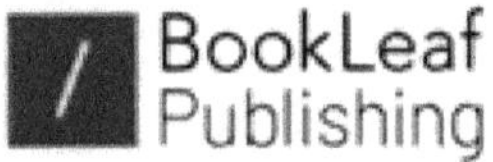

BookLeaf Publishing

Presentation by *BookLeaf Publishing*

Web: www.bookleafpub.com

E-mail: info@bookleafpub.com

ISBN: 9789357211024

First edition 2022